REVIVAL FIRES
IN CANADA

REVIVAL FIRES
IN
CANADA

by KURT E. KOCH, Th.D.

KREGEL PUBLICATIONS
Grand Rapids, Michigan 49501

Revival Fires in Canada © 1973 by Kurt E. Koch is a translation of the original German book entitled *Die Erweckung in Kanada* published by Ev. Verlag, West Germany in 1972. All rights reserved.

First edition.............1973

Library of Congress Catalog Card Number 72-93352

ISBN 0-8254-3015-1

Printed in the United States of America

To my Swiss friends
Ruth and Dr. Arthur Scherbarth of
Bern, Switzerland, and Kelowna, B. C.,
with true appreciation and gratitude.

CONTENTS

FOREWORD

This record arose from the prayers of several prayer groups in Saskatoon, where the revival in Canada began.

On June 7th, 1972, Pastor William McLeod wrote to me: "We are praying that God will equip you with the Holy Spirit. We must remember that the Lord fills only vessels which are empty. This truth was a great blessing to myself some time ago. Water always seeks the deepest level. So too the rain of God's Spirit always flows into the deepest regions. The truth expressed in this illustration applies also to our pride and arrogance. Only the humble are visited by the Holy Spirit."

The following account of the revival in Canada is not complete. There are several reasons for this. Firstly, the revival is still moving; it is in the process of extension. Every week new areas are being added in which God's Spirit is lighting a fire. The second reason for the incompleteness of this account lies in the fact that I am never able thoroughly to visit all the towns and villages in which God's fire has begun to burn, although I have often travelled through Canada.

I must therefore ask all my brothers and sisters to forgive me if there are things missing in this book which are important to them. Much more has taken place than is recorded here.

I would also like to thank the ministers who have provided me with material or allowed me to speak in their churches. Most of all, I am deeply grateful to the brother and sisters who remember my work in their prayers.

Chapter 1

LAND AND PEOPLE

Canada is a fascinating country for the visitor from Europe.

We who dwell in the Old World are to a greater or lesser extent, consciously or unconsciously, victims of an "insular disease." Our land is too small. We feel shut in. Everybody is breathing down his neighbor's neck. We are prisoners of living space. We rub and chafe one another. We tread on each other's corns.

Is it surprising that many long for more room, for more peace and quiet, and cast wistful glances over the ocean?

Canada is a focal point for all those who want to emigrate. It is the second largest country in the world, covering about ten million square kilometers. If that does not mean much to you, consider a few comparisons.

This one country is as big as the continent of Europe and two million square kilometers larger than the continent of Australia. The area of West Germany would fit 40 times into Canada. And yet Canada has only about 20 million inhabitants. In the space in which one Canadian lives, 120 people have to live in West Germany.

A single country, Canada will stand a number of comparisons with the continent of Europe. If we held a kind of geographical quiz between Canada and Europe, Canada would come out of it very well. The longest river in Europe, the Volga, is 3694 km. long. The longest river in Canada, the Mackenzie River, stretches 4063 km. from its source to its estuary. The Alps would fit more than ten times into the Rocky Mountains. And Mount Logan, with its height of 6051 meters, overtowers Mont Blanc of the Alps by about 1200 meters. But this naive geography game is not what matters. The giant country of Canada stands at the beginning of its economic development, whereas for "old man Europe" not many chances and possibilities remain open.

The extent and natural power of Canada's land mass is not her only advantage. The European animal-lover, who in his homeland never has the opportunity of coming face to face with a bear or elk, encounters a wealth of fauna in the Northern forests of Canada. Once a black bear crossed my path only four meters away. On another occasion a little bear-cub cried out in terror as I made my way into the undergrowth. I have taken photographs of elk at close quarters. I have unintentionally startled red deer. The almost endless forests, which cover up to 43% of Canada's surface, give one with their untamed power the impression of another world which we in Europe no longer know.

The population is a colorful mixture of races. 50% are of Anglo-Saxon origin. About 30% are of French descent. The rest are made up of Germans, Japanese, Chinese and many other races.

My own personal interest centered not on the settlers but on the original Indians. There are still about 150,000 of them. Added to these are about 10,000 Eskimos. The mysterious ties binding these peoples to nature are a fascinating subject for study.

We civilized peoples think ourselves so educated and knowledgeable, and yet as far as the knowledge of nature is concerned we are such novices.

The climate of Canada is very varied. The polar region is the home of the polar bear, the caribou and the musk-ox.

Further South comes the forest zone, an Eldorado for hunters, fishers — and for the camera.

Then, after the belt of lakes and a second belt of forest, is the great wheat-growing area with its continental climate. Canada exports 75% of its corn to feed the hungry masses in India, and even in Red China.

The climate is divided, however, not only in a North-South direction, into polar, sub-polar and temperate zones, but varies from East to West as well.

The Eastern coast of Canada is washed by a cold water stream which flows from the Davis Straits southward. This means that Newfoundland, New Brunswick and Nova Scotia have long, hard winters. Even as far inland as Montreal there are ground frosts at night until mid-May.

The West coast is warm and damp. On Vancouver Island the ground is only frozen for about two weeks in January; that is all the winter they have. On the other hand, the West coast has a very high rainfall.

Every part of the country, whether it is cold or warm, has its own advantages. Thus East Canada has a great fruit-growing area in the region around St. Catharines.

In the west the Okanagan Valley has developed into a centre for tourists. Visitors are drawn here by lakes, mountains, forests and huge fruit plantations in the region of Kelowna, and also by the healthy climate.

Canada offers much variety. Though I have been over it fourteen times in twelve years on my lecture tours, I cannot boast that I have a thorough knowledge of this enormous country.

The portrait of the land would be over-optimistic if I were to make no mention of its problems. There are tensions between the different language groups of settlers. In Quebec the French-speaking and English-speaking communities are often at loggerheads. On the West coast, in the Vancouver area, the Germans sometimes feel that they are downtrodden and underprivileged.

Such minority problems exist, however, in every part of the world, with the laudable exception of Switzerland, where three language groups live together amicably.

There are, however, other problems which are more serious. Canada has a relatively high proportion of mentally disturbed people. I was surprised at this, for the average Canadian is healthier and more balanced mentally than his neighbor in the United States.

One Canadian psychiatrist, who attended the congress of psychiatrists and psychotherapists in Vienna, said that about one Canadian in eight had some kind of mental trouble.

A teacher in Vancouver painted a different picture of the situation for me. He said that 40% of the school-children were in need of psychotherapy.

I am familiar with this problem of an increase in mental disorders, but I am unable to account for the high incidence in Canada. The process of neuroticization is quite intelligible in the United States, but up to now I have been unable to discover the causes for this development in Canada.

There are other facts which I find even harder to understand. In the province of Quebec a friend supplied me with the following information. The government has given the Satanists — members of a "church" which worships the devil — a grant of

$35,000. That is approximately £15,000. The reason stated for this support for the Satanists was their social work. State grants are made out of money from taxes. And that includes the taxes paid by believing Christians! Funds from Christians for practicing Satanic cults!

A single case, just one little stone in the mosaic, throws a spotlight on other abuses.

I know a Christian couple with ten children. They are not only churchgoers, but people who pray and read the Bible with their children.

In the neighborhood lived a 23-year-old divorced woman, who made advances towards the 13-year-old son of these Christians and seduced him. The father soon realized what was happening, and forbade the boy to have anything to do with this lustful woman. The boy would not obey. Thereupon the father punished the boy. The son went off to the local youth department and reported what had happened.

Several days later a youth worker from this department appeared. He was a young man with long hair and untidy clothing, dirty and foul-smelling from head to foot.

This youth worker, evidently predestined for uncleanliness, tried to explain to the father: "The behaviour of your son is the fruit of the religious instruction you have given him. The boy ought to be taken away from you."

The youth department applied for a court order to withdraw the boy from parental care. The judge agreed and made the order. The boy was given a home with an unbelieving family. Now he may continue to visit the divorced woman and have intimate relations with her. That is modern education, which is regarded as better than the prayerful concern of the parents for their child.

This case has been checked out in every detail. I was present myself when the father, furious, brought this crying injustice before a member of the parliament in Ottawa, Mr. Richard Thompson. The Member of Parliament, who is a convinced Christian, promised to look into the case.

Such incidents happen today in every country of the Western world. Long-haired, atheistic, communist fellows, who are themselves inwardly confused, can become social workers and youth officers. And these scruffy individuals are then "education experts", who claim to know more about education than Christian parents who are bringing up ten children with much prayer.

This is the situation of the last days. 2 Tim. 3:1-4 is today being fulfilled more exactly than ever.

Chapter 2

THE RELIGIOUS FACE OF CANADA

The settlers brought their own churches with them. The French settlers at the beginning of the sixteenth century had Catholic Priests and Missionaries in their train. For this reason Canada is today still forty percent Catholic.

The English settlers for the most part used the Anglican rites for their services when they came to the New World. The Protestant groups are the strongest. They make up fifty percent of the population. Among the German settlers, it is the Mennonites who have maintained longest their national identity. After ten generations the Mennonites still speak German, whereas settlers with no religious ties lost their native language in the second generation.

After the Mennonites, it is the Baptists who have kept the strongest sense of religious national identity. A number of well-known Baptist ministers make it their definite aim to preserve the German language and German customs in the organization of their churches. An example is Pastor Gebauer of the Pilgrim Church of Vancouver. Pastor Babbel of Kelowna, B.C., goes even further, in that he conducts

not only all the services in German, but also the
confirmation classes. In this way the children of
German families receive instruction in the German
language. Babbel often has six or seven hundred
people attending his services.

The general impression Canadian church life gives
to the visitor from abroad is one of everyone building
his own little kingdom. Each small group —
sometimes only fifteen people — builds its own
church. In 1962 somebody in Kitchener told me, "For
every thousand inhabitants, Kitchener has one
church."

There is something to be said for decentralization.
Mammoth churches are certainly not ideal. But the
other aspect of this fragmentation is the desire of
every minister and every council of elders to gather
as many church members as possible. This habit of
proselytizing has many disadvantages, of which I
have often become aware. It is very difficult to
arrange inter-church meetings, because every minister wants to preserve his own little flock.

The following incident will provide an example of
what I mean. In Montreal I spoke at morning service
in a well-attended church. The minister refused to
announce my evening address in another church.

This state of affairs is made even clearer by a
letter which I received. A doctor who moved to
Canada twenty-five years ago wrote and told me: "I
have difficulties in my spiritual life which are
probably up your alley. I cannot go to a Canadian
pastor, because he will at once try and get me into
his church. The majority of Canadian ministers are
not concerned with building the Kingdom of God, but
with attracting new church members. I would
therefore like to ask your advice in Germany."

What a distaste for this seeking of new church
members it reveals, when a doctor asks the advice of
a minister in another country.

The spiritual strength of the various churches differs very much from place to place. There are pulpits from which anything but a biblical gospel is preached. I have met ministers who visit spiritist seances, or who belong to Masonic Lodges or to the Communist Party. The modern theologians, too, have only rationalistic "pearls of wisdom" to offer their congregations. Preachers of this kind can give their churches no spiritual food. They are putting hindrances in the way of their hearers.

In the midst of this spiritual desert there are also oases of spiritual life: disciples of Jesus, who in weakness and yet with authority, hold forth the Word of life.

In the four hundred years of Canada's history, however, there has been no nation-wide spiritual awakening.

This era is now coming to an end. At the present time Canada is experiencing a spiritual revolution reaching from the West coast right over to the East.

Chapter 3

THE BACKGROUND OF THE REVIVAL

Many revivals, but not all, have a previous history. God can send revival without any difficulty. But very often he responds to years of praying and pleading for a spiritual renewal.

In the last few decades in Canada there have been groups of people praying for a revival, and they are continuing to do so. I would like to mention some of these groups and individuals by name.

One spiritual center which God has blessed is the Prairie Bible Institute in Three Hills, Alberta. This has always been open to spiritual and biblical movements. For this reason they invited Duncan Campbell from Scotland to minister to them. Campbell was the leading man in the revival in the Hebrides.

This man of God was shocked at the moral degradation of the Canadian people. He prayed earnestly for a revival in Canada. One night when Campbell was again on his knees praying for Canada, he had a vision from God. He summed it up in a single sentence: "I saw Canada on fire from coast to coast".

Among fanatical groups, visions are today a luxuriant, rampant field of weeds. For the most part they do not have their source in God. Campbell's vision was a genuine one. He lived to see the beginning of the revival in Saskatoon, but died a few months later.

From another quarter, as well, the believers were called upon to pray for revival. Ernest Manning was Prime Minister of Saskatchewan province for twenty years. He is a believing Christian. In 1966 he sent out over the radio the message that all Christians ought to take the opportunity of the Canadian centenary to unite in prayer for a revival. Many listeners to his program took him at his word and did so. Today Manning is still a Senator, and the messenger of the radio program called the "Back to the Bible Hour."

In spite of the cold climate in many churches in Canada, there was a large number of small prayer cells and individuals whose heart yearned for a revival. One of these, for example, is Lee Bryant, who wrote the book *"Come Fill the Cup,"* and his group of friends.

There were also individuals who were so convinced of the necessity of a revival that they had no rest over the matter. For instance, Pastor Phillip Grabke of Saskatoon told me how William McLeod had for two years avoided all unnecessary work and spent his time in intensive prayer for revival. It was in this man's church, the Ebenezer Baptist Church, that the fire of revival first broke out. McLeod was also a friend of the late Duncan Campbell. We will say something more about him.

Chapter 4

WILLIAM McLEOD

In May 1972 I got to know of the work of the Rev. McLeod in Saskatoon. He is a humble man and does not want his name to appear in this book. The spiritual awakening in Canada is, however, an event in the history of the Church which must be recorded in detail. Secondly, this revival must be preserved from the shifts of emphasis which have unfortunately already found a place there. It is therefore essential that the dates and the circumstances should be firmly established.

Bill was born in 1918 and grew up in Winnipeg. His mother belonged to a Presbyterian church, and was a woman of prayer.

After his education in primary and high school, he worked for his living down a mine, digging up potash. A few years later he was out of work and travelled through Canada looking for employment. He returned home at the age of twenty-two, without success and thoroughly discouraged. In his disillusionment he picked up a Christian book. It was about the return of Christ. Bill became alarmed. He knew that he was not ready. The many prayers of his mother were answered. At the age of twenty-three Bill was converted to Christ. This brought his unemployment to an end. He went from one mining camp to another, preaching the gospel of the Saviour of sinners. He spent four and a half years in this evangelistic work.

Perhaps we have noticed in this story that the young man became a missionary and a preacher without any theological training. A Baptist Church employed him. In this period as an official pastor, the Lord led him in some wonderful ways. One day he went to visit a member of his church who was ill. It was a woman who was in the last stage of cancer. She had already developed secondary growths. The doctors had given the patient up. Bill showed the woman the plan of salvation and prayed with her, in obedience to Jas. 5:14. As he was praying the sick woman saw and felt the hand of the Lord. Bill himself saw nothing. The woman was healed instantaneously, and left the hospital, to the amazement of the doctors. As for the young pastor, this answer to prayer greatly strengthened his faith.

In 1963 Bill took over responsibility for the Ebenezer Church in Saskatoon. Here one day he had an experience similar to that in his first church. A man was brought to him who had been confined for fourteen years to a wheel chair. The man was so weak that he was not able even to hold up his head. After a long period of counselling, the pastor again prayed with the patient in accordance with Jas. 5:14. A week later, the man was well and no longer needed a wheel chair. Two years before the beginning of the revival God prepared His servant. It was a process, a school in humility.

In the Kingdom of God there is a principle that only those who are weak and totally broken experience God's power. The Lord adorns the humble with victory (Ps. 149:4).

The closing incident of these two years of schooling was a remarkable experience. Bill had a dream. He

saw the hand of God approaching him. It touched him.
This touch brought him sharp pain. Finally he cried
out: "I can no longer bear the pain." Then the Lord
opened his hand. In it was a lump of gold as big as an
egg. He was given a word from Job 23:10: "He knows
the way that I take: when he has tried me, I shall
come forth as gold."

Two weeks after this dream Bill experienced a
mighty empowering from above. Four weeks later the
great revival of Saskatoon and Canada began, in his
church.

I am very grateful to the Rev. McLeod for giving
me this window into his spiritual development. We
spent six unforgettable hours together on the way
from Saskatoon through Winnipeg to Minneapolis. It
was indeed the result of God's gracious leading, that
we both had to fly to Minneapolis on the fifteenth of
May, 1972. Bill had to speak for three days at the
Bethel College in Minneapolis. I myself had to conduct
a seminar for ministers and church workers on the
subject of counselling and the occult.

Almost everywhere in Canada there is an atmosphere of revival, and already it has spread to several
areas of the United States. The seminar was attended
by more than six hundred people. In Europe it would
never be possible to get so many ministers to spare
the time for such a gathering. This also is a fruit of
the revival.

Chapter 5

STRONGHOLDS FALL

The human heart is deceitful above all things and desperately wicked, says Jeremiah (17:9).

One of the hardest of human bulwarks is the pride of the white man.

It was at this point that the revival in Saskatoon began. People began to realize that they had sinned greatly, and to break down and confess their pride.

How did it begin?

Pastor McLeod had invited the twin Evangelists Ralph and Lou Sutera to come and speak. I do not know much about this pair of Christian workers. They are reserved when it comes to talking about themselves. The only thing that I know is that they had a very active mother, who devoted a great deal of time, money and energy to God's kingdom. Very early in their lives the two sons were taken out with their mother, when she went to distribute tracts in the streets or to visit people. Unlike the Rev. McLeod who had no training, Ralph and Lou went to the Bob Jones University, which is at present located in Greenville, South Carolina.

The evangelistic meetings began on the 13th October, 1971, in the Ebenezer Church. After a few

days there was already an amazing spirit in the
meetings. The hearers were gripped by the spirit of
confession. After the address, people pressed to the
front of the church to confess their sins publicly. It
created a great impression when the twelve counsellors, whom the Rev. McLeod had prepared for this
evangelistic campaign, were the first to come out and
humbly admit the sin in their life.

The number of people attending these meetings
became so great that parallel meetings were held in
larger churches in Saskatoon. But even the great
church of Pastor Walter Boldt, the University
Alliance Church, was quickly overfilled. Two further
churches were then used, and finally the great Civic
Auditorium. Altogether about three or four thousand
people came to hear God's word, with a spiritual
hunger in their hearts. Under the power of the Holy
Spirit, the people to whom God had spoken lost the
sense of time. The evening meeting sometimes went
on until 1 a.m. After the main meeting, many stayed
behind to an after-meeting for counselling. In the
Canadian revival this is known as the "after-glow."

The people taking part in the after-glow sit
together in a circle and discuss their particular
problems. Then these matters are prayed over. If
anyone needs individual counselling he goes with a
counsellor into another room. These after-meetings
sometimes lasted until 4 a.m.

The need for sleep, the sense of hunger and
shortage of time became completely secondary
matters under the working of the Holy Spirit.

Here are a few examples:

Pastor McLeod invited all the ministers of the City
of Saskatoon to a Ministers' Conference in order to
discuss possibilities of working together. The conference began at 10:30 in the morning. This meeting too
was visited by the Spirit of God. They forgot their
engagements and all the usual duties, and stayed

until five o'clock the next morning". In other words they were together under the Word of God and in prayer for 18½ hours. Similar stories are told by taxi drivers. The taxi firm often received calls for cars after midnight. The customer would then ask to be driven to a church.

The taxi driver would say, "But there aren't any churches open at this time of night." "Oh yes, there are. I have not taken leave of my senses. I want to get right with God."

The driver would then discover to his surprise, light in the windows of several churches at one or two o'clock in the morning.

A similar experience was told me by Pastor Richard Grabke of Portland, Oregon, in the U.S.A. He was interested in finding out about the revival and for this reason flew to Winnipeg. He asked a taxi driver to drive him to a church. The man told him: "This town is all upside down. The most extraordinary things are happening. Criminals are giving themselves up to the police. People don't want to do anything but sit in the church. We are called out at night to take people to church in the early hours of the morning."

"Good, then drive me to a church as well," answered Pastor Grabke. And he was not mistaken. The driver brought him to a church which had been gripped by the spirit of revival.

The leaders in this God-sent movement have been careful not to count the numbers of those converted. The number remains one of God's secrets. In the whole country, however, there are tens of thousands who have come under the influence of God's Spirit.

Rigid fronts of church tradition have been shaken. People who were sure of themselves have found the ground taken away from under their feet. All human authority has broken down. Pious conceit has been unmasked, hatred has turned into love. All who have

been touched by the Holy Spirit have begun their
lives for a second time.

Chapter 6

PASTORS AND CRIMINALS

God is no respector of persons. Before His blazing holiness there is no place for self-assertion.

Even Isaiah, the great prophet of God, cried out when he encountered God: "Woe is me, I am lost" (Isa. 6:8).

Many Christian workers who stand on the side-lines have no share in the flood of blessing. There is a symbolic word about them in Ezek. 47:11: "But the swamps and marshes *by it* will not become fresh" (Luther). This verse once came alive for me in a sermon which I heard in the Free Church in Bern. In every revival there are people who stand on the side-lines, when God is going through the land. The most amazing things can take place nearby, but if we are standing on the side-lines we are not drawn in. And that can be a serious sin.

In the revival of Saskatoon both "high and lowly" were touched by the spiritual tidal wave. We should not forget that it was not the high priests standing at the foot of the Cross whom Jesus took into Paradise, but the robber who was at the Lord's right hand. I can give an example of a similar happening.

There was a criminal who was being hunted in

three Canadian provinces on a variety of charges. He
had already spent fourteen years in prison. His raids
and the constant need to flee from the authorities
brought him to Brandon. For some inexplicable
reason he went to a Christian meeting. There his
conscience was touched by the Word of God. He
spoke with a counsellor and surrendered his life to
the Lord. On his own initiative he went to the police.
The man at the station asked him, "Why are you
giving yourself up?" The criminal replied: "I have
found the Lord Jesus here in your town, and now I
want to follow Him. That is why I am giving myself
up." His confession was accepted and passed on along
the usual channels. What happened was quite
unexpected. Because of the way he had acted, he was
released. He brought his wife and three children over
from Ontario and for the first time began to enjoy a
peaceful family life.

Ministers too can be "caught." While Pastor
McLeod was preaching in a certain church, another
minister, who was sitting in the congregation,
interrupted and said, "Stop for a moment. I am on my
way to hell if I do not at once confess my sin and
accept the Lord Jesus." Bill stopped in the middle of
his sermon. The minister came forward and openly
confessed his sins. In general we should be very
cautious about public confessions of sin. In times of
revival, however, people are gripped by such a fearful
sense of sin that they cannot help confessing it
publicly.

Another minister told me his own story. He was
strongly opposed to his daughter, who was leading a
scandalous life. He was even thinking of giving up his
ministry. Then, under the preaching of McLeod, he
became so aware of his own sin that he, and then his
wife too, had to repent. The next morning he got up
in front of his congregation and asked them publicly
to forgive him for all the things he had neglected. In

his own family, too, everything changed. The daughter came to Jesus and said: "The life and attitude of my parents has changed so radically, that I felt myself compelled to begin my life again with Jesus."

It is encouraging that a pentecostal preacher in a Baptist Church had a decisive experience. He was a man who claimed to have received the baptism of the Holy Spirit. Under the preaching of an evangelist, he broke down despite all his pride. He came out and confessed his sin. When he went home, his wife and children were amazed at the change that had come over him. He had been a father whose outbursts of rage had terrified the members of his family for years. Now this devout wolf had become a lamb. "If anyone is in Christ, he is a new creature. Old things have passed away; behold, all things have become new." (2 Cor. 5:17).

A minister who had been trained at university was touched by the spirit of the revival. His whole past came back before his eyes, and terrified him. He could find no peace until he had informed the university that he had cheated in his final examination and thus gained the diploma by false pretense.

Those ministers whose life and work had passed through the filter of the Holy Spirit then became a blessing to their whole churches.

Chapter 7

ABSOLUTE STANDARDS

McLeod told me in the course of a personal conversation, "The chief characteristic of this revival is love." People who previously could not stand one another have embraced each other and asked for forgiveness. Ministers have become reconciled with their co-workers. In all kinds of human relationships the sand has been removed from the works. Love has become the basis upon which all questions are settled.

A woman who had been active in church work for a number of years admitted to me: "I could not stand our minister's wife with her blunt manner. Since the revival I have found such love coming into my heart that I can love this woman from the bottom of my heart."

The atmosphere of love among the newly converted has become so powerful that people who were inwardly torn apart and in despair can find rest and peace there.

One evening a care-worn woman turned up in the after-meeting. Nobody knew what was going on in her heart. She sat there in silence. She asked no questions and gave no answers. One or two people started to pray particularly for her. This went on until four o'clock in the morning. Then the ice broke. She confessed that she had thoughts of suicide. The previous evening she had said to herself: "This is my last attempt to sort myself out. If it doesn't work this time, I will make an end of it all".

Sometimes the reconciliations were quite dramatic. In one church there were two leaders in the choir, who had been in extreme opposition to one another for years. Not only that, but they were in fact brothers in the same family. I know them. I was staying in the home of one of the brothers when he told me about the change which had come over his life. How did they come to be reconciled? The evening meetings are of a very informal character. There is not always a sermon from the evangelist. Sometimes they just have "testimony evenings," in which anyone is allowed to tell of an experience he has had with the Lord.

On one of these evenings one of the brothers went to the front and repented. His first action after this was to go to his brother and ask him for forgiveness. His brother made no response, but remained unmoved and unapproachable. Then the penitent brother asked Pastor McLeod to help him with the problem. Bill beckoned to one or two of the leaders, and then went downstairs with the two brothers. There the Pastor spoke to the hard-hearted second brother. His exhortation and entreaties were without effect. After twenty minutes he had got nowhere. Then Bill said, "We shan't get anywhere like this. Let us pray about it." The elders, the brother who wanted to be reconciled and Bill went down on their knees. Fifteen minutes later the spirit of repentance came over the second of the brothers. He became so strongly aware of his sins that he jumped up in despair and knocked his head against the wall, crying out: "O God, is there still any hope for me? Can my anger and hatred still be forgiven?" That very hour the two brothers came to one mind. Love had triumphed over hate. Together with their wives, the two men went up, knelt down on the platform and repented. Tensions that had existed for years were overcome.

Another story about a choir-director is even more amazing. Again I ought to say that I know this brother well. I heard his story in his own house.

This choir-director, who was of German extraction, had been a trouble-maker in the church for many years. One Sunday morning the minister confessed that God had opened his eyes concerning all his misdeeds and asked the congregation to forgive him. This annoyed the choir-director. "Why do we have to have all this exaggerated nonsense?" That was the opinion of this refractory brother. But his hour was to come. One evening this man went forward and confessed his sins. Then he went to his minister and asked him to forgive him for all his opposition.

The repentance of this choir-director and the complete surrender of his life to Jesus was to bear fruit in many ways.

He was employed as an engineer in a potash mine. One day there was some trouble on a conveyor belt in a seam a thousand meters below ground. The engineer was given the task of repairing the fault during the lunch break. When the transmission had stopped, our friend set to work. The repair took longer than had been expected. The lunch break came to an end and the foreman came back. For years it had been the job of the foreman to press the button and start up the conveyor belts again. This time he forgot. When the engineer looked at his watch, he was startled. The break had already finished sometime before, and he was still in the middle of the great machine .

He would have been crushed as he worked on this

repair if the foreman had pressed the button as usual. When the two men met, the foreman said: "Someone was looking after you, or you would no longer be alive." This miracle of deliverance had further results. When the mechanic realized that the Lord had preserved him from this terrible death, he said: "Lord, I have eight more days of holiday to come, and I am giving them to You. Send me out with a team to the place where You want me to be."

The plan was carried out. Together with several brothers he decided to travel to Winnipeg and work in one of the churches there.

Before they started out he tried to telephone a minister whom he knew. But he was unable to get through. All the same, they set off with the intention of trying another call while they were on the way. They were still about sixty miles from Winnipeg when the group again dialed the number. Again there was no reply. Then the four men prayed together for a little while. When they had finished, the minister whom they were seeking drove into the car park.

"This is extraordinary!" said the brother from Saskatoon as he greeted him. "We have been trying to phone you from various places and have been unable to get through. And here you are in front of us."

"It is just as much of a puzzle to me. I had not planned to come out here this afternoon. But I had such a strong feeling within me, that I had to come here."

"This is a remarkable piece of guidance. We are looking for a place in Winnipeg where we can say something about the revival in Saskatoon and preach the gospel."

"And I am most interested in what you have to say," continued the Pastor from Winnipeg. "That is probably why the Lord has led us together.. The human wires failed, but God's telephone worked."

The brothers from Saskatoon now had the invitation they needed, and continued their journey.

A new problem developed. As they drove on they heard a grinding noise in the transmission of their car, which got louder and louder. Shortly before they arrived in Winnipeg they looked for a place to get it repaired. They asked the chief mechanic to repair the car quickly because in a few days they had to return. They took the opportunity of speaking to him about his salvation as well.

Despite all these difficulties, they finally arrived at the church of this pastor in Winnipeg. The first evening they held a meeting. The Spirit of God was moving in this gathering.

In this church the engineer again experienced the guidance of God in an unusual way. Without noticing it the speaker, who is of German descent, used the German language. Not until he had been speaking for ten minutes did he notice his mistake; then he continued in English. This mistake was again part of God's plan. In the service there were some old people who had come over from Germany after the last war. They could understand little English, and were very pleased to hear the gospel in their mother tongue.

At the end of the evening about thirty people went to the front and surrendered their lives to the Lord Jesus.

At the end of their evangelistic tour in Winnipeg, yet another surprise awaited the brothers from Saskatoon. When they went to collect their car and asked for the bill, the man replied, "It has all been paid already."

"How so"?

"What you said to me about my need to make a decision for Christ is payment enough. I will give you the cost of the repairs."

The engineer returned to Saskatoon full of thanksgiving and praise. The series of miracles had begun with his deliverance in the machinery down the mine, and it had ended with the payment of the bill for the damage to the transmission of his car.

Between stretched a chain of blessings from the Lord. This shows how God is able to mingle natural and supernatural, and bring everything together to form a meaningful whole. As we follow Jesus, wonders never cease.

Chapter 8

RADICAL HONESTY

The second characteristic of the revival is absolute honesty. Everything which is high and lofty is humbled. All pride is shattered. "Honest to God, honest to my neighbor" is one of the watchwords of inward cleansing.

Pastor McLeod told me that sometimes people were prepared to pay a hundred or even a hundred and eighty dollars (£ 40 — £ 70) for a telephone call, in order to make their confessions. Nor did it make any difference to these callers what time of the night it might be. Pastors had to be ready around the clock to receive a telephone message.

Honest to God — that applied first of all to those whose work involved them in continual use of the Word of God. Professional familiarity with "holy things" may result in the minister's sanctification, but it can also make him worldly, and blunt his cutting edge. Thus one pastor confessed publicly before a great crowd of people: "I am a hypocrite."

A missionary opened up and said: "I confess my jealousy. I was jealous because the revival did not come to my church, but in the Baptist Church." This wave of "honesty to God and honesty to one's neighbor" also touched many voluntary church workers. Elders of the church admitted that they were continually criticizing, even despising, their ministers.

Solicitors, psychologists and professional men of every kind accepted Jesus and repented publicly or in private. It was not a case of confession with the lips only. Inward correction followed.

One farmer, for instance, went to his neighbor and said: "Jorg, I have stolen a cow from you. Please forgive me. I will replace her."

The neighbor replied: "You need not replace her. I stole one from you as well. Please forgive me too."

A social worker confessed that he had stolen goods from a warehouse and paid back what they were worth.

A customs officer confessed his dishonesty with dutiable goods, and paid damages. Another thief declared: "I have stolen, but I cannot repay what I have taken."

Swindlers came back to inns, restaurants and hotels, admitted that they had gone away without paying, and paid their bills.

A man who had cheated his insurance company said to his boss: "Please give me a free afternoon today. I have something urgent to attend to." Then he drove to a place sixty miles away, confessed the fraud to his insurance company and paid up what he owed.

College principals had students coming to them and revealing the devices they had employed to trick the examiners in order to pass. The teachers in the colleges and the lecturers in the universities declared that the atmosphere in their institutions had changed fundamentally since the beginning of the revival. Instead of protests and rebellion, the pupils and students were engaged in reading the Bible. It was as though the problems of authority, which had previously appeared insoluble, had all at once been blown away.

I asked the Rev. McLeod: "Bill, what sort of sin was most frequently confessed?" He replied: "Arrogance, self-seeking and pride. Before the revival people used to say, my home, my car, my firm, my business, my garden. Now, since this wave of cleansing and expropriation, everything has been handed over to the Lord. Everything belongs to Him. He has the supreme right of possession, and the sole power to decide."

Chapter 9

HEALINGS AND DELIVERANCE

We live at a time when drug addiction is growing as never before in human history. Mankind is becoming ripe for the judgment of God.

Anyone who has to work in the field of social welfare and youth leadership knows about the most hopeless struggle against the wave of drug addiction. Doctors, psychologists, ministers and judges find themselves helpless in trying to ward off the dangers of addiction.

What is impossible to man, God has done. The word still applies: "If the Son makes you free, you will be free indeed" (John 8:32).

On the twelfth of May 1972, I held a youth evening in Bill's church. Radiant faces, free people! A number of them had been slaves of drugs, and had become free in the revival. In the last ten years it has become evident that only the power which comes from God can effectively free those who are bound by drug addiction. The courses of treatment prescribed by doctors and ordered by judges are good. But experience shows that ninety to ninety-seven percent later returned to addiction. Only what Jesus does is lasting in its effects.

One of the best examples is the experience of Lee Bryant, whom we have already mentioned. By an act of God He was freed from the bondage of drugs and of alcohol.

I have often been asked, in the course of my travels, whether healings also took place in the revival area. The revival of Saskatoon is a movement of repentance and cleansing. Healings have not been given prominence. But they are taking place all the time in answer to prayer. We must never forget that the salvation of a man is more important than the healing of his body. When this is forgotten, we fall into an unbiblical, extremist position.

Some of these healings ought to be recorded. There was a boy who was totally deaf in one ear. The specialist advised an operation. The parents gave their consent. At the same time some people who were praying were notified. They began to pray for this boy. Shortly before the operation was due, he was healed of his deafness. It thus became unnecessary to operate.

There was a man who some years ago had suffered injury to his spinal column. Since then he had been in terrible pain. The pain-killing medicines which he took had little effect. In the revival he surrendered his life and his troubles to the Lord. Others prayed with him, and he experienced a sudden healing.

Even more widely known and miraculous was the healing of a schizophrenic woman. For years she had been in the hands of psychiatrists. She had been given thirty electric shock treatments. She had to take about twenty pills a day. The doctors did not know what to do with her. But the Lord touched her and healed her completely. This woman is now a living testimony to the grace and power of God to help and to put us to rights.

The many healings of neurotic and depressed persons tell a similar story. They are simply the result of the tremendous joy which came over people who had been touched by the Holy Spirit. This statement must not be misunderstood. Not emotionalism, but joy. Joy in the Lord overcame the miseries of life as it had been.

Chapter 10

THE REVIVAL SPREADS

Every revival spreads. What was originally the revival of Saskatoon is today a movement affecting the whole country.

The Rev. McLeod and the Rev. Walter Boldt and many other ministers and brethren have been invited to preach all over Canada and U.S.A. There are many people elsewhere who want to share in the blessing which the Lord has to give. For this reason I, too, made several attempts to go to the revival area. I succeeded, as this record shows.

Let us not however begin with the ministers. It is sometimes more impressive to see how the Holy Spirit uses unknown Christians as His implements.

A truck driver from the province of Saskatchewan came through Saskatoon and was there touched by the revival. He experienced a clear conversion to Christ. One weekend the firm gave this driver a load to take to the U.S.A. On Sunday morning he was driving his truck through a small village when he noticed that people were crowding into the church. He made up his mind to park near the church. Then he went into the service, dressed in his working clothes.

The minister saw the truck and said to the stranger: "You have a Canadian license from Saskatchewan. Do you know anything about the Saskatoon revival?"

"Sure! I myself made a decision for Christ there."

"Can you tell us something about it?"

"I am willing to do that."

"You have only half an hour. We must finish the service at eleven o'clock."

The driver began his story. When eleven o'clock came, no one looked at his watch. He went on. The hearers even forgot their dinner. Only the mothers with small children went out. The others stayed. One o'clock passed, then two o'clock. The whole church was gripped by the Holy Spirit. The first person to be affected was the minister himself.

At 2:30 the service came to an end. It was not the minister who set the time limit, but the Spirit of God. This truck driver was one of the first to bring the spirit of the Canadian revival to the U.S.A.

This experience was also the fulfilment of a dream which the truck driver had had before he set out from Canada. He had told his mother: "I had a dream, and saw myself preaching to the people in a church." This vision had thus been fulfilled, although the driver was not a man of outstanding intelligence.

The fires of revival came to Eastern Canada when Pastor McLeod was invited to the Central Baptist Seminary.

Perhaps this is the place to point out once again that revival cannot be brought on by men, even if they are gifted evangelists. It is only the Holy Spirit Himself who can create new life.

Bill spoke in the Seminary in the morning. The Lord evidently desired to visit this theological college with the breath of the Spirit. Students and faculty alike forgot their mid-day and evening meals. The meeting lasted until past midnight.

From all over the place came requests and calls for a team to be sent. For example, a long-distance call from St. Louis came to Saskatoon. A negro pastor asked: "Can God really revive a dead, defeated, sin-saturated church?"

This negro brother had at least a clear insight into the needs of his church.

The radiations from the Saskatoon revival touched first of all many towns in the same province.

Regina is an example. Here there developed a news center for the revival. The monthly magazine "Revival Fellowship News," has increased its circulation twentyfold in six months. This is an indication of how hungry people are for spiritual renewal. Just to mention the most important of the new centers which have developed: Winnipeg, Brandon, the Okanagan Valley, Vancouver, Thunder Bay/Ont., Portland/Oregon (U.S.A.) and many others.

Hundreds of teams went about lighting the fire of the revival like bearers of the Olympic flame. After the revival had broken out in Winnipeg, sixty teams were formed in the first few weeks from this city alone, and are now engaged in travelling around the country.

It looks almost as if the Holy Spirit wants to bless and to use this team system in a special way.

In Germany, for example, Wolfgang Heiner began with a team. In the Indonesian, revival groups of students went out every weekend as teams.

In the Canadian revival this system has again appeared to be very fruitful.

The twin evangelists Ralph and Lou Sutera, who are being used more than anyone else in the Canadian revival, form, of course, their own team. It is a repetition of the pattern in Luke 10:1: "The Lord appointed seventy others and sent them on ahead of Him, two by two, into every town and place where

He Himself was about to come."

This book was already finished when a "stop press" report reached me from Kitchener. It comes from Nick Willess, whom I met at the Saskatoon Airport.

He writes: "Our meetings here in Kitchener have gone well. The Sunday morning service lasted until two o'clock. The four o'clock meeting went on until ten o'clock in the evening.

"When the altar call was made, the Moderator of the Church went out and declared that the leading men of the church should first of all give their lives to the Lord. Thereupon all those who had some part in the leadership of the church got up on the platform.

"Moderator, pastor, deacons and elders knelt down and surrendered their lives afresh to the Lord. After we had prayed with them, I asked the congregation whether others wanted to join them. About seventy of those present followed their example, came to the front and gave over their lives to Jesus. Because a great deal of discord had reigned in the church, the church members prayed also for a cleansing and a new consecration of their church.

"A Moslem, who was married to a Christian woman, also came into the church, after his wife had confessed her failings to him. He said goodbye to Mohammed and accepted Christ.

"When we left Kitchener, we went away with the conviction that we were leaving behind many whose lives would never be the same as before!"

Chapter 11

THE VALLEY SPILLS OVER

The valley spills over. So said the "Revival Fellowship News." To which valley does it refer? The answer is, the valley for which I have prayed more than any other in Canada, the Okanagan Valley. In April and May, 1971, I gave lectures there in five different churches. I came to value the believers there highly, but not only them, for the scenery is also very beautiful. I am often in danger of becoming a nature-worshipper. But I always look beyond the creation to the Creator.

The Okanagan Valley has its own characteristic features. From Pendikten, past Kelowna and right down to Vernon, stretches a narrow lake about three times as long as Lake Zurich. Parallel to the Eastern and Western shores run ranges of hills. Behind these are higher mountains, like, for example, Big White, a well known ski resort. On both sides of the lake there are large plantations of fruit trees. As I have already mentioned, it is an area which has developed into a tourist center because of its natural beauty. This valley with its many villages was touched by the revival when Ralph and Lou Sutera came to evangelize. It was my intention to visit the Okanagan Valley a third time, but I was unable to fit the visit into my schedule.

Thus I received the following letter from my friend Henry Dyck, the minister of the First Mennonite Church: "First of all, peace be with you. Out of the abundance of the heart the mouth speaks. That is how it is going with us in Kelowna at the moment. It has pleased the Lord to send revival in this area. We have, of course, long been praying for it. But we did not dare really to expect it, for Kelowna is stony ground. Some pastors confessed that they had prayed for it but did not believe that it would come. Now the Lord has done it in spite of our unbelief, and we just stand all amazed.

"As I am writing this letter, the text for the day reads: 'The wind blows where it will.' That is once again coming true. The Pastor of the M.B. Church has experienced a renewal along with seventy members of his church. In our church too, there is more life. In Grace Baptist, Pastor Babbel said: 'Since the founding of this Church nothing like this has ever been known in its history'. Other churches have similar stories to tell. The ministers have been torn right out of their usual routine. They have to learn to get out of the way of our Lord, and then watch from the roadside how He is working.

"This truth is also emphasized by the two brothers Ralph and Lou. They say: 'We have to make room for God.'

"It must also be mentioned that the 'tongues' movement has no place in this revival. It does not even come under discussion.

"I must tell you about another very interesting matter. It happened in the Wood Lake Elementary School. I heard of this incident from the mouth of a minister who has experienced spiritual renewal through the revival.

"His eleven-year-old son goes to the school I have mentioned. During a break time he watched a group of children playing with a ouija board. (Author's note: the ouija board is a dangerous, spiritualist game.) The eleven-year-old had been warned about this game by his mother. In his presence the children asked the ouija board: 'Who gives you your power?'

'Hitler!' came the reply.

'Come on, don't treat us like fools. Tell us the truth!' The letter board answered: 'Lucifer'.

The children did not understand the word, and asked: 'Who'?

The ouija board then replied, by way of explanation: 'Satan.'

'At this moment, the eleven year old boy, whose parents had been affected by the revival, went up to them and said: 'In the name of the Lord Jesus I condemn you!'

"The boy came home and told all this to his parents.

'What do you think happened'? he asked. 'The game suddenly stopped. The board would not work anymore. But that was not the only thing,' continued the boy. 'After it had happened, another boy told me, 'If there is so much power in the name of Jesus, I will start coming to Sunday School in the Church. I want to hear more about this Jesus.'

"I listened to this story very carefully, for I have been working for the last six months in this school. All these events prove that the Light is driving out the darkness.

"To God be the glory."

This letter from Henry Dyck reminds one of the verses of Psalm 8: "Out of the mouths of babes and sucklings hast Thou ordained strength".

Let us not however speak only of Kelowna. Forty miles south of Kelowna is Penticton, which I also know from my own travels. From there a Christian worker wrote me the following letter: "I am so happy about all the reports of the blessing which has come through the revival breaking out all over the place. Perhaps we are at the beginning of a Worldwide revival.

"I retired here in order to spend my last years in peace and quiet, a time filled with self-seeking pleasures. My eyes were opened to the fact that I was squandering my retirement with worthless, unimportant things. Now the Holy Spirit has given me an X-Ray test, and revealed all the things which were wrong. He then brought me to a new surrender of my life to the Lord and made me put my 'retirement' at His disposal."

Here is another testimony from the Northern end of the Valley, the town Vernon, about 35 miles north of Kelowna. The Lutheran Pastor Rude — incidentally a German name of the Peace Lutheran Church, writes as follows:

"Our morning service began at 10 o'clock. A team of five brothers reported what God had done in their lives. While they were speaking the spirit of repentance came over the meeting. After our guests had given their testimony, I read various reports about the revival in other towns. I also told them what I had heard from other ministers. When I had finished, I called on all the members of the congregation who were present, in total about 175, to come down to the front. I asked them either to devote their lives anew to the Lord Jesus, or to make a decision for Christ for the first time. Many responded to the challenge and came out. They knelt down, and I knelt likewise in the midst of them, to surrender my life once more to the Lord. At the end, the church was filled with the songs of praise of those who had been touched and blessed by the Holy Spirit."

I have an original letter from another Pastor in

Vernon before me. It is dated 23rd January, 1972, and reads:

"Today I want to tell you about the death of an old pastor. I am the man! It was a painful experience and lasted a terribly long time, before I was finally ready. But life on the other side of death is fantastic. It is nothing other than the fact of Jesus now living in me and through me. I am certain that Christ will succeed in directing and moulding my life according to His will."

Is it not about time that we two said goodbye to our old man and crossed the 'death line'? Then we too would have a share in this wonderful revival, which God is sending to Canada at the present time.

Chapter 12

VANCOUVER

This metropolis, on the Western Coast of Canada, has a population of one million and is the most important Canadian port on the Pacific.

I cannot write about the revival in this city without remembering those with whom I am linked by prayer.

I have stayed in this city eight times in all, and given addresses in many churches. For this reason I would like to take this opportunity of thanking all those who have given spiritual support to my work: Walter Hannemann, Pastor Gebauer, Ernst and Dorle Koltzenburg, Eva and Jakob Rempel, the Jeske family, Mrs. Klein, Mrs. Krause, Rev. Birch and many others. I am thankful that they have been allowed to witness a wonderful revival in their city. I would count myself fortunate if I had been able to have some part in it. When I gave twelve addresses in Montreal in May, 1972, Dorle Koltzenburg's sister told me:"My sister must have experienced wonderful things in Vancouver. For four weeks she and her husband never got home before midnight." The working of the Holy Spirit was stronger than any bodily need. It is a great joy to me that in revealing His power and glory God has not overlooked the

German minority groups in Vancouver. The German
pastors, Babbel of Kelowna and Poswatta of
Winnipeg, came to minister to the German churches.

The movement in Vancouver began like that in
Saskatoon, through the ministry of the Sutera
brothers, Ralph and Lou. On the first Sunday, 5th
March, 1972, the Ebenezer Baptist Church was filled
to overflowing with more than 2,000 people. The next
Sunday there were 3,000 people gathered in two
churches. The revival which followed spilled over into
other churches. After a few weeks five churches were
full.

The present-day evangelists in Europe have
something to learn from the Canadian system. The
campaign in Saskatoon lasted seven weeks. In
Vancouver it went on for two months. The same is
true of Portland, Oregon, of which we will hear
presently.

Our evangelistic weeks, with six meetings, are not
thorough evangelistic campaigns, but only "warmers
up."

The effect of these weeks of preaching in
Vancouver was to bring life into all the aspects of
church life. Weekly prayer meetings, which before
the revival had been attended only by a small group,
swelled. In one prayer meeting there were 75 people,
in another 150. The weekly women's meetings in one
church reached an attendance figure of 450. The first
lunch-time meeting for men brought together 250.
Moreover, this revival spread, as it had done
elsewhere, in cells across the land. Thus the ministers
of White Rock, B.C., wrote: "We are holding for the
time being a daily prayer meeting, until we can get
an evangelist or a team."

Another pastor, in his hunger for personal
blessing, twice travelled 265 miles in order to have a
part in the Vacouver revival. Afterwards he wrote a
report:

"For years I have been longing for a genuine revival. It seemed as if a sense of defeat was reigning in the hearts of Christians. Then I heard of the revival in Saskatoon and in Vancouver. With great hopes I came from Ohio, U.S.A., to this beautiful city. The days went by so quickly and now I am on my way home again.

"How can I bring home to my church the remarkable experience, which one has in the revival area, of having to take one's seat an hour before the service begins, in order to get one at all? How can I describe the atmosphere, the excited expectancy which people have there? The church feels as if it were electrically charged.

"No description can convey the overwhelming sense of sin which gripped one young man. In the middle of the service he cried out: 'Can't someone pray with me, so that I can get right with God?'

"The hearers were in a spirit of great awe and expectancy, or even filled with a realization of their sin which put everything else out of their minds.

"It is just as hard to convey the character of the after-meetings. They lasted until the early hours. People who had been convicted by God declared what wonderful things the Lord had done in their lives. Young men and old were tested and cleansed in their innermost being by the Spirit of God. Their testimonies reflect this experience. I will never forget the tears of joy when people found peace. Nor can I forget the realization of victory, and the filling with God-given love, in the lives of those who previously had had no contact with the Lord.

"And so to this city and to all my new friends I say farewell. By the grace of God it is not a farewell to the revival, but the beginning of God's work in my heart".

Chapter 13

GRACE FOR BACKSLIDERS

In the news-sheet of the Alliance churches, "Midwest Memo," I read an astonishing advertisement. This notice is all the more significant because the paper is published by the District Superintendent of the Alliance Churches. It read: "Martin Bowker, a backslidden preacher, who was restored to full fellowship at 3:30 a.m. in a Saskatoon meeting, has been used by God in meetings in Moose Jaw and Weyburn and is available for further revival meetings." A backslidden pastor had returned! A few years ago I was struck by the words of Hosea 14:4, "I will heal their faithlessness; I will love them freely, for my anger has turned from them." Grace and mercy for the faithless and backsliders. I have mentioned Martin Bowker because he has toured Eastern Canada as an evangelist. The Lord is using him as His messenger.

Toronto, Kitchener, Waterloo, Hamilton, Burlington, St. Catharines and Ottawa are some of the stops on his route. He even had an invitation from Puerto Rico. At the moment Pastor Bowker is staying in Laos and Cambodia and ministering to missionaries.

This shows that the Lord can take a life which has

become spiritually worthless through faithlessness and idleness, and fill it anew with His grace.

The revival fires are burning in these Eastern districts of Canada. First of all let us mention Ottawa, the seat of the Canadian Government. Many believers pray particularly for their government and all the Members of Parliament. Their prayers are not in vain. Richard Thompson, leader of the Conservative Party and a Member of Parliament, has begun a prayer meeting together with his colleagues. Eighteen Members of Parliament take part.

From the steel town of Hamilton came the following report: "At a prayer meeting on 13th January, 1972, Rev. Bowker gave us the first impression of the revival. When he challenged people to make a decision for Christ, many came forward. We sensed the presence of God. When the meeting had ended, most of the people did not go home but stayed together to talk about their problems."

A brother in Hamilton who had been going to church for twenty-one years as a believing Christian, but had never been able to pray in public, was touched by the Spirit of God. His tongue was released, and he developed a rich life of prayer both in private and together with other Christians. In the prayer meetings in other places in Ontario healings took place, although these were not stressed. It was a natural, unsensational matter, just simple answers to prayer.

Toronto, too, was touched by the revival. I have already recorded the experience of the Rev. McLeod in the Theological Seminary of the Baptists. Now I want to relate just a little about a church in Toronto. About two years ago the pastor had invited me to speak at this church. He was not only a talented but also a spiritually-minded brother. My talks were attended by several hundred people. Unfortunately I discovered a peculiar attitude among the elders. I will give no details. The pastor resigned from this church two weeks after my visit. When I heard of the revival in this church, I wondered whether these elders had been affected by it. It is quite possible.

If a backslidden pastor like Martin Bowker could find the way back to Jesus and now works amid such blessing, then God can also deal with church elders. On the other hand it often happens that, in a church which has been touched by the revival, not everyone is affected by the Spirit of God. This was something I found in many places. People who called themselves Christians can stand by, cold, unaffected, sometimes even hostile, while others are gripped by the Holy Spirit.

Chapter 14

A CHURCH LEADER

Church leaders have greater difficulty than other people in finding the way to Jesus and to a Spirit-filled life. This fact is demonstrated both by history and by the experience of the present day. Harms, Volkening, Blumhardt the elder, Henhofer, Modersohn and many others all had problems with the Church authorities. A spiritual brother, Oberkirchenrat Werner de Beer, once said to me personally, "When I became a member of the High Consistory, I lost my spiritual power. When I had become so disgusted with it that I resigned, my spiritual authority returned."

Why is this? There is no one pattern underlying this state of affairs. Often those who are theologically "over-enlightened" are just the ones who are spiritually "under-enlightened." Intellectual pride is a barrier against the Holy Spirit.

Perhaps it is sometimes due to the way in which these people are appointed. Superintendents, prelates, members of the High Consistory and bishops are often chosen for their ability and intelligence rating, or even for their excellent manners. Their own capabilities then all too easily form a blockade against questions of revival and personal, spiritual renewal.

I am all the more happy, therefore, to be able to follow my report about Martin Bowker with one about a senior church official.

Pastor Grabke gave me a duplicated circular letter. It had been written by David Clink. He is the Executive Secretary of the Baptist General Conference for the Canadian Prairies, a man of considerable influence. This is his own report, although I can give a shortened version only.

"Five days after the beginning of the evangelistic campaign, I arrived in Saskatoon. At that time I did not yet know that God had begun to work in a wonderful way in the lives of the people. Actually I ought to have expected something of the sort. Pastor McLeod, who has been working now for nine years at the Ebenezer Church, had for a long time been an example to me, and was all that a pastor should be. Bill boasted no other education than his time at High School. Since he himself felt the lack of a good training, he asked God for the ability to learn parts of the Bible by heart and to be able to quote them correctly. I see in Pastor McLeod the key to the present revival. He gets up regularly at six o'clock in the morning, goes into his study without having any breakfast, and spends the whole morning in prayer and Bible study. He himself did not foresee this revival. In the last few months he had shortened his program of visiting in order to have more time for prayer.

"On Monday the 18th of October, 1971, I went to my first meeting, simply as a spectator. I did not notice that the revival had already begun. To begin with I sat right back in the last rows. Later I went further forward, in order to watch the people who were praying or giving their testimony. I was skeptical, but I watched carefully.

"At midnight I got up to go. But Ralph Sutera stopped me with the words: 'I see that the District Superintendent is here. It would interest us to know what Brother Clink thinks about all this.' For a moment I was taken aback. I did not want to say I was against revival, because I am not. But I doubted whether what the people were saying was true. Everything went on in an orderly manner. No one tried to whip up people's emotions. Exaggerated utterances occurred occasionally. But everything proceeded in good order, although there was no program.

"In answer to the question I said something like this: 'I am glad that God is touching people's lives. For years I have prayed for a revival, preached about revival and longed for revival.'

"When I had spoken, Brother Sutera thanked me for my honesty. But I was not so honest as the evangelist thought. Then Brother Sutera called several men who were standing nearby, and asked them what they thought about what I had said. At this late hour of the night, or early hour of the morning, there were still about forty people in the church. The men asked me several pointed questions, intended to expose what it was that held me back from being a Spirit-filled man. I desired a renewal for myself, but I did not want to go down to the depths of which these people were speaking. I was afraid of being humbled and of confessing my sins, as I had heard others do.

"I left the church and went to the after-meeting. At about four o'clock in the morning I went to the house of Pastor McLeod, where I always stay when I am in Saskatoon. I was very tired and wanted to do nothing but sleep.

"The after-meetings were held after the main meetings in private houses. Their meaning is a kind

of group therapy; people who need help from God
talk it out in small groups. Their problems are
discussed and prayed over.

"I withstood the meetings until   Thursday evening,
the fourth day of my visit. When the invitation was
given to make a decision, I went forward. I knelt
down and waited a long time for someone to come
and speak to me. Probably it was difficult for the
leading brethren to find someone to counsel the
District Executive Secretary. Finally Dr. Brock, who
had led the singing every evening, came over. He has
written and composed about five hundred songs.
After he had prayed with me for a while he said, 'I do
not feel qualified to counsel you.'

"Thereupon I went into Pastor McLeod's study. At
that time I did not know that all the members of
Ebenezer Church were praying for me. When a newly
revived church prays for someone there is no hope of
further resistance.

"My last visit that Thursday night was to the
after-meeting in the home of Brother Gateint. There
were about twelve people there: the McLeod family,
the two Suteras, Dr. Brock and one or two others.
They asked me several questions. We had a
discussion about the problem of self-love and of being
filled with the Holy Spirit.

"We got no further. Then someone in the circle
asked me to put my chair in the middle of the circle.
This is the usual method of 'group therapy.' I did it
and then knelt down. Several of them, or all, prayed
with me and for me. They asked God to break down
whatever stood as a hindrance in my way. It was now
already five o'clock in the morning and I was still not
touched. Dr. Brock declared: 'There must be some
barrier. My advice to him is: go into a room and
battle it out with God on your own.'

"The group then went home, and I lay down to
sleep. After a short while the Lord woke me up

again. I was ready at last to clear out of the way the hindrances which I had recognized, and to do what God demanded of me. In the days and weeks that followed I had to ask several people to forgive me; wrong things had to be put right again.

"There were financial matters, too, to put in order. Reparations had to be made. It was a deep-going experience for me. The next night, when I went to bed again, I had to ask the Lord: 'Lord, cut off a bit of my joy, otherwise I shall not be able to sleep.' This was not my experience alone. Others who had been touched in the revival went through exactly the same."

How grateful I am to Brother Clink for his open testimony. It is good that the Holy Spirit brings leading churchmen low, and has no respect for titles. Even men of authority in the church can really be saved.

Chapter 15

YOUNG LIVES GIVEN TO GOD

In the Saskatoon revival about forty per cent of the people who have been changed by the Word of God are young people. This is a fulfilment of a verse in Amos 2:11, "I raised up some of your young men to be devoted to God." The youth problem is very acute today throughout the world. Problems include a generation gap, drugs, sex, despondency, deadly boredom, anarchy, rebellion, insubordination. Psychologists, teachers and theologians are almost all helpless when faced with the growing chaos.

There is one place where these problems are overcome and healed. That is when young people are put right in the sight of God. By way of example I will give a short account, which could be multiplied many times.

From the 12th to the 14th of November, 1971, some youth groups of the Baptist Church were holding a weekend retreat in Springside, Saskatchewan. The leaders of these groups had come to the point where they no longer knew how to cope with the problems of the young people.

The organizer of this youth camp heard, before the

weekend began, of the revival in Saskatoon. On an impulse, he telephoned to Saskatoon to find out more about it. He considered whether he ought to drive with his wife to the revival area, although it was two hundred miles away.

The two of them prayed about it, and God encouraged them with the words of Isa. 43:19, "Behold I am doing a new thing; now it springs forth, do you not perceive it? I will make a way in the wilderness and rivers in the desert." On the Wednesday (November 10th), they set off to take part in the meetings in Saskatoon. Then they drove back, and began to organize a second trip for Thursday together with the young people. They packed three cars and arrived in time for two meetings.

Eight of the young people were moved by the spirit of the revival. They gave their lives to the Lord. After midnight they drove back to Springside and arrived there at 6:30 a.m.

There were only two hours left before school was due to start. Although the young people had travelled four hundred miles in twenty-four hours, they were so full of joy that no one noticed that they were tired.

Their witness went round the school in one day. That was the beginning of a revival among school pupils and teachers.

The same evening the campaign began. There were about two hundred young people taking part. It took a different form from that planned by the leaders. The program that had been prepared was abandoned. The eight young people who had received Jesus the night before gave testimony to their experience.

The spirit of repentance came over this great congregation of young people. Many of them came forward to dedicate their lives to Jesus. Those who had made the same decision only twenty-four hours before helped to counsel them. That weekend nearly eighty young people made a decision for Jesus.

Let us hear what one of these new converts has to say. He is a student in the University of Regina.

"A few months ago I had a great, fantastic experience. It did not shatter the world. But the world became different for me. Perhaps you have heard of the week-end camp for young people in Springside. Fortunately I was taking part. After we registered we were first of all shown a film. I thought: a good opportunity to take a nap. So I made myself comfortable. But instead of sleeping, I began to give attention to the curious film. The film was not nearly as stupid as I thought at first. It contained a message. When I heard it, I found myself in a strange mood. I began to reflect about religion, about God and about myself.

"The next day I had already begun to take more notice. The testimonies and experiences which I heard people relating did not impress me particularly. They only had the effect of making me feel like a poor good-for-nothing, a miserable failure.

"I had of course been successful in sports, but that could not guarantee my eternal life.

"By Friday night I had already shed a few tears. But Saturday was God's day for me. First of all I heard a few more stories of people's conversion. They touched me to the depths of my soul. But the devil held his dirty hands in between. He kept on whispering to me: 'Keith, this is not for you.' It was a hard battle in my heart. Finally I confessed my sins to God and put everything into the balances. My pride was broken. My friend Wayne came up to me and said, 'I love you in the Lord Jesus,' that was all that was needed.

My self-control was at an end. My old man collapsed. Tears flowed, not tears of sorrow and pain, but genuine tears of joy, joy in the fact that we could feel the presence of God and of the Holy Spirit.

"On the third day, Sunday, I gave my testimony. Previously I would never have been able to speak out about my life to people who knew me. But God had put a new power in me.

"Many people say it is hard to be a Christian. But is that not the reason why we have been given the most powerful book, the Bible? Does that not bear witness to the mighty power of God; to Him who forgives our sin and surrounds us with His love? All that we have to do is to take one step towards God. He catches us and draws us near. He never leaves us. God can become a reality for us, *your* reality just as He has become *my* reality."

Chapter 16

THE CHILDREN OF GOD

On the 15th of May, 1972, my host, Philip Grabke, seemed very upset over a youth meeting which had been planned. The following day a large group of "Children of God" was due to come to Saskatoon. I was unable to understand his concern.

The so-called "Children of God" are an offshoot of the "Jesus People". In Europe they had been given a good write-up in the Christian press, because of their name.

The expression "Children of God" enjoys a good reputation among believers in the Old World. In our younger days our ministers taught us the verse John 1:12, "As many as received Him, to them gave He power to become the children of God, even to those who believed on His name."

Why then this anxiety in the revival area? I had yet to learn about them. During one of my many journeys through North America I acquired a report put out by the Inter-Varsity Christian Fellowship.

This missionary organization, which works particularly among students, is biblically sound. The report is based upon authentic experiences with the "Children of God" and has come as a shock to many.

On the 1st of July, 1971, a meeting took place in Montreal between a group of "Children of God" (who also call themselves "Prophets of Doom") and some senior Protestant youth leaders. The staff of "Youth for Christ" also took part in the consultation. The matter being discussed at this meeting was the urgent question of how one can help young people with their drug problems and the epidemic of rock music.

A few days later the director of "Youth for Christ" and several of his staff were persuaded to leave their organization and to join the Prophets of Doom. One of them, a man of 22, telephoned his parents on July 4th to say that he was leaving "Youth for Christ" and was going to live in a secret place. He had given his life totally over to the Lord Jesus. The same pattern repeated itself in various towns of Eastern Canada. Young people from definitely Christian groups gave up their parents and all their friends, and joined the "Children of God". Many girls also flooded into the new movement. Naturally this development aroused suspicion among many parents, although the Prophets gave the impression of a deep spiritual life and study of the Bible.

The father of the former director of "Youth for Christ" in Montreal travelled from the U.S.A. to Belleville in Eastern Canada, to look for his son who had disappeared. He found his son's address, and his son was at home, but he would not speak to his father. After waiting without success for five hours, the father travelled home again.

He consulted a lawyer and then returned to Belleville on the 21st of July, where the young man was brought out to meet his father by order of the chief of the police. A widely known Canadian evangelist spoke to the young man for four hours, in the presence of his parents. It was all to no avail. The young man was absolutely stubborn. The expressions

he used indicated that he had turned to extreme
views. He spoke of his Marxist friends, of revolution,
of the rotten state of all the churches and of his
hatred against society.

After this the disappointed father collected all the
information he could about the "Children of God".

He discovered that the headquarters of this splinter
group of the Jesus people is situated in Texas. The
center goes under the name of the "Texas Soul
Clinic".

These Prophets of Doom direct their efforts
particularly towards Christian young people. They
say to them: "Our standard of Christianity is very
high. Perhaps it will not suit you". All those who
become members of this movement are given some
training and are kept under strict supervision. They
are not allowed to leave the house or even to go to
the door without their body-guard.

If any one is still uncertain as to what these
"Children of God" stand for, one fact should
completely open his eyes: The leader of the Prophets
declares that he is God. All members receive from
him a "baptism from above." After this baptism they
can live and act exactly as they like. Boys and girls
live together. There is no privacy any more. Here we
see once again a fulfilment of what Paul says in 2 Cor.
11:14, "The devil disguises himself as an angel of
light."

No wonder then that in Saskatoon, the center of
the revival, the coming of the "Children of God" was
viewed with some apprehension.

This means, therefore, that when Christian papers
in Europe give a favorable report of the "Children of
God," they are making a grave mistake.

Chapter 17

PSEUDO-CHARISMATIC
MOVEMENTS

It would be better for me if I did not have to write this chapter. The reason I say this is the fact that unbiblical groups will use every means to defend their position. Every revival encounters opposition in the form of disturbances. Satan does not quietly look on when people come in crowds to repent and give their lives to Christ.

Opposition comes both from the extreme right and from the extreme left. The extremists on the left are the rationalists of every kind: Modern theologians, liberal critics, wooden upholders of orthodoxy. They are the theological fire brigade who cast doubts upon everything and throw water on the fire.

Those on the extreme right are emotional groups of many kinds. They over-emphasize the feelings, and concentrate too strongly on the third article of the Creed. They deal in gifts of the Spirit, and confuse psychological reactions with the working of the Holy Spirit. Moreover, they often stand in opposition to genuine revivals.

The same tensions are to be seen in the revival in Canada. Several ministers in the revival area said to

me independently that the Pentecostal Churches had
not been touched by the revival. Individual Christians
from these groups, who themselves held moderate
views, came to meetings in the other churches and
were gripped and changed by the revival. The
Pentecostal Churches themselves, however, remained
outside the stream of blessing.

I am sorry to have to report this. The truth,
however, must be placed on a lamp-stand. And now
for one or two experiences of this kind. In one church
a couple came to me for counselling. They confessed
that they had up to now belonged to a Pentecostal
Church. The husband had received the laying on of
hands by a Pentecostal preacher five years before. As
a result he had been healed of an organic disease.

At the same time, however, he felt himself
emotionally and nervously burdened. His love for the
Bible and for prayer also diminished. Such transfer-
ences of organic complaints to the psyche are not
biblical healings.

Mrs. Grabke told me of the following experience.
She was a witness of the revival in Winnipeg. While
she was standing among the people who were
repenting, working as a counsellor, a woman came up
to her and said: "The Lord has shown me that He
wants to bless you with the gift of speaking in
tongues." Mrs. Grabke answered: "I do not desire this
gift."

The same Pentecostal woman made her presence
felt in other ways as well. She entered into the room
at Winnipeg where lay helpers were counselling
people. She was taken to be another helper. She
created confusion by telling the women that they
must have the gift of tongues, for otherwise they
would not be in a state of full salvation. Pastor Brock
then informed Pastor McLeod of the incident. Similar
things happened in Saskatoon, the place where the
revival started. In the churches which had been

touched by the revival, people appeared who spoke in tongues and demanded that believers should have this gift as evidence of their baptism in the Spirit. The believers, however, after some hesitation and questions at first, quickly recognized the unbiblical position of these false teachers, who turn the gifts of the Holy Spirit into legalistic demands. It is remarkable that in the great revivals of this century in Korea, Formosa, and Timor, the Holy Spirit passed the Pentecostal Churches by.

Perhaps one incident in particular throws a still clearer light on the charismatic movement. I confess that originally I myself was in favor of this movement, before I saw its exaggerated effects and legalistic narrowness. The charismatic movement operates on a basis of psychological experiences, mediumistic gifts, and suggestion — and is far from being charismatic. There are of course in this movement genuine, faithful Christians, who unfortunately do not possess the gift of the discerning of spirits.

Now I come to the example I mentioned. I was told of this incident by a minister. P.B. was a Methodist preacher who lived and worked in Saskatoon. His son had a serious and incurable disease. A famous man from the charismatic movement, whom I know very well, came to give a series of addresses in Winnipeg. The Pastor went with his sick son. The healer laid his hands upon the patient, with the words, "The Lord Jesus has healed you."

A few months later, a report appeared in the magazine, "Charismatist", about the healing of the young man from Saskatoon. The father wrote to the healer and pointed out: "My son has not been healed; his condition is worse." In spite of the letter, the same untrue report appeared again a few months later. The father was angry and wrote again to the healer. A year later, the healer again related the same story in a radio message.

This time the father wrote in stronger terms: "I am writing to inform you for the third time that my son has not been healed. He has in fact now died. If you report this so-called healing once again, I will prosecute you." That did the trick.

A single incident like this can never, of course, be used to condemn a whole movement. In every church and fellowship there are faithful people of God and also scoundrels.

The healer whom I have mentioned anonymously in this chapter has been known to me for twenty years. He has performed many "healings" of this sort.

To complete the picture, another example of this man's work. Again the story comes from a believing minister. The charismatic movement was organizing a series of addresses in Denver. The speaker was the above-mentioned healer.

After one of his addresses a boy was brought to him, whose leg and hip were held by splints which the doctors had given him. The patient had been ordered to wear the splints for six months. Then they were to be removed.

The speaker held an after-meeting for those who were sick. He came up to the sick boy, and declared him healed in the name of Jesus.

Then he asked the person with the boy to remove the splints. It was done. The healer declared: "Now take a few steps". The boy obeyed and made one or two steps in great pain. When he left the meeting, the boy who had been "healed" collapsed. He was taken to the hospital. The doctors told him "We cannot put right the damage which has been done by the premature removal of the splints."

Healers of this sort nearly always say, of course: "Well, you did not have enough faith; that is why the trouble has become worse."

The parents of this boy have not kept quiet about it. The "healing that went wrong" became public knowledge within two days. The population was so incensed that the healer had to discontinue his series of meetings.

This "charismatic" movement has nothing to do with a genuine biblical revival.

We need to be clear-sighted in order that we may learn to distinguish what is genuine. The Holy Spirit opens the eyes. Emotionalism obscures the differences.

Chapter 18

THEOLOGICAL KNOW-ALLS

Revivals are also exposed to extremists on the left. If feelings are the ruling consideration for the "extremists on the right," the group of the left gives the supremacy to reason and human understanding. The expression "extremists of the left" is open to misunderstanding, because under it are lumped together liberals, neo-rationalists, upholders of a rigid orthodoxy, and theological anarchists. On one matter they all speak with one voice: "There is no such thing as demon possession. He who speaks of it only proves his own theological and philosophical naivety."

In the revival area Pastor McLeod told me: "Since we have had revival, many cases of possession and demonization have come to light." The same observation was made by the Rev. Richard Grabke, the leading brother in the revival of Portland, Oregon.

I put the question: Why do the Professors of theology not go and study a revival by spending a considerable time in an area which has been visited and blessed by God? It could happen that the Holy Spirit would reach the conscience and the mind of a theologian and completely "turn him around." Theologians know, of course, from their theology what a revival is, even if they have never come in contact with it in their lives. A summary judgment of this kind, which completely misses the mark, is to be found in Professor Thurneysen's book *"Seelsorge im Vollzug."* Page 231, translated in English, reads: "All these speculative portrayals of a spirit-world are characteristic of the other-worldly longing to be found in all revival movements."

What revival has Professor Thurneysen experienced? Switzerland has had no revival in the last 70 years. Was Professor Thurneysen ever in the revival area of Korea, Uganda, Formosa, Indonesia, Asbury, the Solomon Islands or Canada? No. Where, then, has he acquired this knowledge of "all revival movements" of which he speaks?

The chief characteristic of revival movements is not another-worldly longing, nor speculation about the spirit world, but recognition of sin, repentance, forgiveness and new life. In short, re-birth through the Holy Spirit (John 3:3), without which no one will see the Kingdom of God.

We may search in vain for this message in the book of the Theologian, Professor Thurneysen, and yet this is a book intended to give guidance to counsellors.

Let us proceed to the chief cause of offence, demon possession.

Anyone who is familiar with my books, e.g. *Christian Counselling and Occultism*, or *Occult Bondage and Deliverance*, knows that they contain warnings about occult neurosis, suggestive symptoms of possession, and possession mania. There are primitive Christians who see possession behind every psychological abnormality.

In all my books I make a clear distinction between mental diseases, emotional disorders, and occult bondage, of which demon possession is the strongest form.

A differential diagnosis is possible, but only for psychiatrists and counsellors who are born-again Christians. A theologian or a doctor who is a nominal Christian, or a Christian by tradition, is not in a position to distinguish the religious facts from the medical data.

I will mention at this point several men who have been given the ability to make distinctions of this sort:

Dr. Alfred Lechler, who was for 35 years the chief psychiatrist at the Hohe Mark Hospital, near Frankfurt. He possessed the medical and biblical equipment to enable him to distinguish psychiatric cases from religious ones.

Professor Rohrbach of the University of Mainz is convinced of the factuality of demon possession.

Dr. Gerhard Bergmann, at present the best-known evangelist in Germany, who takes up on pages 258 and 264 of his book *Und es gibt doch ein Jenseits* the subject of angels and demons, says that demonic bondage does not fit into the psychiatric pattern of depersonalization. Thus he recognizes the fact of demon possession.

My friend Professor Flüge should be mentioned; he is familiar with the biblical phenomenon of possession.

In England mention should be made of the group of doctors led by Dr. Martin Lloyd-Jones. In my presence several psychologists have declared that they had cases of possession which could be distinguished from mental disorders.

In the U.S.A. there is Dr. William S. Reed, the psychiatrist. He has said: "Many psychic and physical disorders are the result of demonic attacks. In modern medicine and psychiatry, therefore, we must take note of exorcism."

Among theologians in the U.S.A. I would name Dr. Fred Dickason, head of the theological department of the Moody Bible Institute; Dr. Myron S. Augsburger,

President of the Eastern Mennonite College; Clate Risley, President of "Worldwide Education Ministry"; Professor Merrill F. Unger, Dallas, Professor Victor Matthews of Grand Rapids and many others.

All these can speak of cases of possession from their counselling experience. Moreover, they are all men who accept my understanding of the evidence.

Professor Thurneysen, on the other hand, says on page 64 of the book we have mentioned: "Since Christ has cleared away the evil spirits, demonology has become demythologized for us." On page 69 he says: "We must certainly take seriously the inner powers, but we are not to believe in their claims to be like God."

What is the background to this kind of theology? To sum it up briefly: "Jesus and his disciples were children of their time. The truth contained in the New Testament is wrapped up in myths from which it is our task to free it." What does Holy Scripture say to this insinuation? Peter declares: "We did not follow cleverly devised myths" (2 Peter 1:16). The New Testament has no need of the demythologization to which the theologians of the 19th and 20th centuries have subjected it. It would be better if our theologians would allow themselves to be freed from their myth of demythologization!

Another insinuation which may be heard today from the side of the theologians is the suggestion: "Jesus and his disciples regarded those who were mentally ill as possessed by demons. Our present-day knowledge of psychiatry gives us greater insight. The Bible is not a medical text-book. We must replace the impression 'possessed' by 'mentally ill.' "

What are we to say to this? The Scriptural answer is simple. In Matt.4:24, Matt.8:16, Mark 1:32, the sick and the possessed are clearly distinguished. In the world of Jesus' day, therefore, sickness and possession were clearly distinguished. The apostles were not

theologically undeveloped simpletons, but men who
had been enlightened and moved by the Holy Spirit (2
Tim. 3:16, 2 Pet. 1:21).

In the face of this weighty and unequivocal
evidence from the New Testament, the statement of
Professor Thurneysen on page 69 of his book is not
very convincing: "A new anthropology has arisen,
which no longer speaks of demonization and
possession by evil spirits."

This "new anthropology" is not that of the New
Testament, but that of the Enlightenment, of
rationalism.

Let us turn again to the statements of the apostle
Paul. In Col.2:15 he speaks of a disarming of the
mythical powers and demons by Christ. But he also
writes to the Ephesians (6:12) that it is not with flesh
and blood that we have to contend, but with the evil
spirits under heaven. In spite of Christ's victory over
the evil spirits, the disciples of Jesus speak of a
struggle and of being attacked by evil powers.

Peter warns us in the same vein (1 Pet.5:8): "The
devil prowls around like a roaring lion, seeking
someone to devour."

What is merely a colorless theory on the level of
theological debate meets us in the area of revival as a
hard reality. We will consider this in the next
chapter.

Chapter 19

STRUGGLING WITH DARKNESS
AT CLOSE QUARTERS

What has been hidden to the wise and understanding, has been revealed to babes, says the Bible. Things which do not penetrate a highly trained theological mind can be grasped in their deepest meaning by Christians who have been filled with the Holy Spirit.

Where revivals are given by an act of God, the devil also tries to find his way in.

Let me begin with an example from Saskatoon. I was told about it by the man I have so often quoted, Pastor McLeod. Shortly before the revival began, a believer, Mrs. B. in Saskatoon, saw in the night a figure coming towards her. She was crippled and could not move. The black figure reached out towards her. Then from the other side came another hand and pushed the black figure away with the words: "She is my child." This brought the attack by the powers of darkness to an end, and Mrs. B. could again pray and move her body.

I am familiar, of course, with the arguments of the psychiatrist and of the psychologist. They would speak of hallucination or of religious projections of unconscious material. And yet medical and psychological arguments cannot explain everything which happens in the realm of spiritual experience.

The next example tells of a tragedy at a Bible school. For about ten years Canada and the U.S.A. have undergone an epidemic of spiritualism which has been going through the schools as well. Millions of young people in North American play with the ouija board. We have already mentioned this practice. This question game has unfortunately appeared even in Bible schools. It is played with an alphabet, a set of numbers, and a pendulum or small glass.

In one of the Bible schools in the revival area the students were conducting experiments with an ouija board. Suddenly below the pendulum they saw a devil's face. They were terrified and ran out of the room. The preacher came and asked them what had frightened them. They told him of their experience and the face. The preacher, who is also a teacher at the school, laughed and said: "We will soon deal with that." He knelt in front of the ouija board and began to pray. At that moment he felt two invisible hands pressing down on his head. He was just as shocked as the students, and in the name of Jesus commanded the invisible powers to depart.

I know the arguments of psychologists about such cases. There is no point in discussing them here, and to do so would need more space than is available in this book.

A well-known fact should, however, be mentioned. We know, for example, from the time of the Wesleyan revival and from the recent revival in Indonesia, that in times of great visitation by God the inward structure of man is open both for good and evil influences. Times of revival reveal the nearness of the Holy Spirit, and at the same time the presence of demonic powers.

That is why at such times of divine blessing many supernatural events occur. When such supernatural experiences are cultivated, as happens in extreme groups, it is an unhealthy thing.

The story of Mrs. B. related above is a true one. In the course of my travels people have often come to me to talk about this kind of problem.

A Swiss evangelist had a similar experience in the Swiss Jura. The unseen world is always interlocked with the world we see, even if in our spiritual blindness we cannot see it or do not want to know about it. At times of revival, when God creates strong points of contact between the natural and supernatural worlds, many individual examples illuminate the close connection between the unseen and the seen.

One thing which was not new to me, but which I had not encountered to such a great extent before, was the linking of speaking in tongues with demonic possession. I am writing here neither in pride, not in malice, but simply in truth.

Various leading brethren in the revival have recounted to me examples of "Tongue-devils." One of the brethren even provided me with a tape-recording on the subject. Let us consider a few examples.

In Edmonton there was an 18-year-old boy who was noticeable at the prayer meetings, because he always prayed in tongues. He was requested to pray in English, so that others might be able to understand. The young man replied "I can no longer pray in English. As soon as I begin I fall straight into tongues." This seemed strange to the brethren. They resolved to test this spirit. When the young man again began to pray in tongues one of them called out to him: "Tell us, you spirit of tongues, whether you confess that Christ has come in the flesh?" That is a test which is mentioned in 1 John 4:1-3. The question was not answered. Then the minister who was present commanded the spirit: "In the name of Jesus we command you, spirit, to pray in English." The command was obeyed.

The people present were terribly shocked when the young man began to utter frightful blasphemies and insults against Christ and against God. Thus in this case the demonic character of the tongues was revealed.

Even more sinister were cases of possession at the Toccoa Bible Institute at Toccoa Falls. There were six cases which were taken down on tape. Personally I do not record such things. It revolts me. However, without asking for it, I was given this tape which had been recorded by a missionary.

I will mention here just one of these examples. There was a girl who often spoke and prayed in tongues. It became too much for those who lived with her. A missionary was asked for advice. He commanded the spirit of the tongues to make himself known. In reply to the question "Do you confess that Christ has come in the flesh?" the spirit cried out: "No, I hate him." The missionary then asked: "In the name of Jesus, tell me how you got into the girl." The demon answered: "By the laying on of hands of a Pentecostal preacher." The whole incident was covered by the intercession of a prayer group. The missionary then commanded this spirit in the name of Jesus to depart. The girl became free and has since prayed no more in tongues.

Since this example could cause much offence, I wish to state again that I believe in all the gifts of the Holy Spirit. In our confused day, when lying powers are declared to be gifts of the Spirit, the subject must however be treated with the greatest caution. I am of the opinion that in the chaos of the last days the fruits of the Holy Spirit probably have even more importance than the gifts. The truth of this is to be seen in the Canadian revival.

It is not my intention by these examples to hurt the humble, faithful, sacrificial Christians who are to be found in the Pentecostal churches. I can easily prove that this statement comes from a sincere heart. I have spoken three times in Canada, twelve times in the U.S.A., eight times in Trinidad, and three times in New Zealand, in moderate Pentecostal churches and Assemblies of God.

It is important to test the spirits and to discern between them with great care. One day, in eternity, there will be Pentecostals in heaven and Lutherans in hell, but the reverse will also be true. It is not we men with our short view who have the last word, but the living and merciful God.

The appearance of demonic experiences was recorded not only in Saskatoon, the center of the revival, but also in the other areas. In order not to have to return to this subject later on I will deal here with the events in Portland. The story of how the revival spread to Portland will be recorded in the next chapter.

My informant for the examples that follow is Richard Grabke, Pastor of the Immanuel Baptist Church in Portland.

A girl came to a counselling meeting asking to be made free. She was an Indian, a half-caste who was involved in Indian magic. She wore pearls as a protection: these formerly were used in a pagan cult as an amulet. She also read regularly the so-called Bible of Satan, although she was a member of a church. She carried magic pearls around with her even when she went to church. At night, too, she put fetishes before the door, to protect her against the evil spirits. These strong demonic bonds did not become apparent until the beginning of the revival. Previously it had all remained unnoticed. Through the ministry of a counsellor and of a prayer group she became free by the help of God.

A great victory for Jesus was the deliverance of a spiritist. Mr. Smith had come from England to

Portland in order to found a spiritualist church there.
He visited several evangelical churches to try and
gather members for his church. When the revival set
in, it "caught" him as well.

He recognized Christ and he recognized his own
position. He repented and surrendered his life to
Jesus. Since then he has been using his knowledge of
the occult for the purpose of warning churches.

The ministry of Brother Smith was, however, still
limited. He was only able to unmask the sins of
sorcery which have serious consequences: but he had
no power to give pastoral advice. One day he came
to Brother Grabke for help. Grabke asked several
other brethren to assist him. A number of weak
points in the life of the former spiritualist and
spiritist were revealed. After pronouncing forgiveness, the brethren anointed him, laid hands on him
with prayer and commended him to the special
ministry of counselling. Since then Brother Smith has
been enabled to minister to the possessed in the name
of Jesus. Out of the spiritist has been made a warrior
of Jesus to fight against spiritism and demonization.

Another example is just as instructive. A girl went
to Bible school, but showed symptoms of possession.
When somebody prayed with her she would lose
control of herself and roll around on the floor. This is
a common phenomenon of resistance, which is
encountered with many possessed people.

Professor Rohrbach of Mainz has had the same
experience with a possessed woman. In Portland a
group of counsellors began to minister to this girl.
When she was again on the floor while they were
praying, they put the girl on a chair, and in the name
of Jesus commanded the demons not to make her roll
around on the ground any more.

They obeyed in the name of Jesus. Then the
brethren commanded the demons to reveal themselves. The command was obeyed. A prayer group

was also present, praying and singing in turns. It is the experience of all pastors who work in this field that hymns of faith, praise, and worship of the Redeemer "get on the nerves" of the demons. Hell fears the glorification of the Man of Calvary and His cross. Prayer and fasting is also a way to victory. In all the cases, however, there is one thing which must not be overlooked. It is not men who can bring help, even if they are the best pastors. The Son of God alone has all power in heaven and on earth. At His command people are made free, like the Gadarene demoniac. This Bible school student was also enabled to experience the triumph of Jesus' victory.

"The reason the Son of God appeared was to destroy the works of the devil," (1 John 3:8). "Thanks be to God, who gives us the victory through our Lord Jesus Christ" (1 Cor. 1:57).

Chapter 20

WINNIPEG

It is 10 years since I held an evangelistic campaign in Winnipeg. Since then I have been linked especially close by prayer with several believers. Among them is Brother Sturhahn, the superintendent of the Baptist Churches, whom I value very highly; also the Koltzenburg family, who now live in Vancouver, and Rev. Walter Stein, who asked me to come at that time.

When you have been praying for a town for ten years, it is not a matter of indifference what happens to the believers there. I have a lump in the throat particularly when I think of a certain matter. A missionary doctor in the Baptist Church regarded hypnosis as justified, and therefore attacked me. I do not force my opinion on anyone.I know that believing doctors hold varying opinions of this question. Personally, because of my own experience in pastoral counselling, I can never rouse any enthusiasm from hypnosis. I was surprised, therefore, to find that in one church this doctor was supported in a vigorous discussion not only by the minister but also by many young people and students who were present. In prayer I am always disturbed when I think of this incident in Winnipeg. This city has now experienced a great revival. I would love to be able to report that the groups to which I preached at that time were involved. In particular I am still waiting for some sign that it has affected the pastor who then took the side of the missionary doctor.

On the 22nd of November, 1971 a team came to Winnipeg and told of the revival in Saskatoon. The report was given to a meeting of ministers. In the time of prayer which followed, the Holy Spirit fell upon those who were present. Tears of sorrow and penitence flowed. The pastors were all overcome by a recognition of their sins. One or two had to ask forgiveness and to be reconciled because of secret rivalry, or jealousy and ill-will.

Many hurried home to put things right with their families. What happened in November, 1971, at this meeting of ministers could be summed up in the words of Luke 19:9, "Today salvation has come to this house."

What the ministers experienced at this meeting, they took back to their churches. Although it was nearly Christmas time, more and more people came to the meeting every evening. Every day between thirty and seventy of the congregation at the services came forward to surrender their lives to Christ.

The first wave of revival came to the English-speaking churches. The Germans understandably desired to have revival meetings in their own language. Something happened which previously would have been thought scarcely credible. Overnight a German evangelical alliance appeared, consisting of twelve churches. They applied to German churches elsewhere which had already been affected by the revival, and asked them for a team to come and visit them. Their wish was met. On the 12th of January a team came from a village 180 miles away. The members of the team told how their whole village had

been changed by the revival. On the very first
evening of this meeting in Winnipeg people surrendered their lives to the Lord. After the second
meeting about thirty people got on their knees and
prayed to God for grace. In spite of the severe
January weather the meetings attracted ever-
increasing congregations.

The following Sunday evening a spiritual break-
through came among the young people. An after-
meeting with about 200 adults and 100 young people
lasted until midnight. In the months that followed the
revived churches in Winnipeg sent out many teams.

This great missionary action has, however, already
been recorded. One of the happiest evangelistic
ventures of this city was when 120 members of the
German Baptist Churches felt called to bring the
message of revival to their old mother country. In
May, 1972, a charter flight to Germany was planned
and carried out.

Chapter 21

REVIVAL IN THE SCHOOLS

Canadian teams pressed forward into the U.S.A. in order to bring the torch of revival there also.

Their reports brought uproar in the Multnomah School of the Bible. In the weekend meetings about a quarter of the students went forward to dedicate themselves to Christ. This wave of repentance and decision caused strong differences of opinion not only among the teaching staff but also among the other students. The school was split into two camps: some agreed with the revival, the others rejected it. The opposition objected to everything: the call to decision, the practice of coming forward and of public repentance; not only this, but the joy of those who had been touched by the revival was described as fanatical and it was said that emotions were being whipped up.

Even so the opposition was unable to prevent the process from continuing. One person confessed that he had cheated in the examination. A doctor confessed his pride. Students learned to overcome their hatred and to be reconciled. A student who had caused his parents much trouble wrote three letters home and asked for forgiveness. Conceited fellows, who had made it difficult for their teachers, became humble. When things of this sort happen, it is not the result of a momentary mood, but it is God's Spirit at work.

Revival is not an intellectual matter about which we should speak once a year, but a biblical fact which we should experience every day. Those who wish only to discuss revival prove that they are not yet ready for revival.

G. Breikkreuz, a lecturer at Merrick Baptist College, tells a similar story. At this school, too, the team from Canada held services. "It is simply fantastic what we have experienced this weekend. My boldest expectations have been exceeded. I must be ashamed of my unbelief. The out-workings of this weekend will be seen in eternity.

"We have 315 students here. More than two-thirds of them have made a decision for Christ. No one would have thought that the Bible could have affected us in this way. We stand here with our mouths open simply amazed.

More than 200 students have now discovered the purpose of life. They are hungry and thirsty for the Word of God and need guidance. It is beyond comprehension. Only a gentle movement of the Holy Spirit, and we have a brand-new school and atmosphere within our walls."

All those who read this report ought to pray for this school, for these students are only beginners in the life of faith. Satan prowls around with all kinds of temptations and lies, seeking to drag back those newly converted.

Chapter 22

PORTLAND

Oregon is the scene of a great revival, approaching in extent what has happened in Saskatoon. Perhaps it is still more far-reaching in its effects. How did it begin? He who begins by speaking of men knows nothing of the plans of God. It was God's will to move over this part of the U.S.A. with the breath of His Spirit. Who are we, born as we are in sin that we presume to say that we have contributed a decisive part towards the revival? At best the Old Testament expression is fitting: *toalath yahweh* = worm of God. A worm lies underground and can be trodden underfoot. We are no more than that in the sight of God.

For the information and material which I have received about the revival, I am indebted to the two brothers Philipp Grabke in Saskatoon and Richard Grabke of the Immanuel Baptist Church in Portland, Oregon. I have stayed with Philipp. I was able to speak to his brother only by means of a long distance telephone conversation. I am planning, however, to make a stopover in Portland on my next flight from San Francisco to Vancouver, since a lawyer has invited me to Portland.

Richard Grabke invited his brother to come and hold a seven-day series of meetings at his church in Portland. These took place between Palm Sunday and Easter, 1972, i.e. the 26th of March until the 3rd of April. When I came to stay with Philipp Grabke on May 11, the meetings were still continuing, although Philipp Grabke had returned to his own church in April.

What had happened in the meantime? More than can be contained in one book. Night after night people came forward to make a decision. Since the crowds could no longer be contained in the Immanuel Baptist Church, parallel meetings were held in other churches. Here too people lost their sense of time. The after-meetings continued until 4, 5, and 6 o'clock in the morning, and once even until 2 o'clock the following afternoon. People of all stations in life were gripped alike by the Spirit of God. Some fifty ministers repented and found God's cleansing for their ministry. Several thousand people who had previously been no more than nominal churchgoers surrendered their lives to Jesus.

One biblical motto dominated: "Allow Jesus to live in you." Professional men laid aside their pride: doctors, psychologists, professors, teachers, public officials, missionaries were touched by the spirit of repentance and surrendered to Jesus.

All the rivalries between the denominations were buried, and bridges were built. Young people who had been in bondage to drugs, alcohol and promiscuous sexual behaviour were made free. People with emotional and mental disorders, who had received electric shock treatments, were healed.

Would-be suicides were filled with a joy which put everything else into the shade. Business men had stolen goods returned to them. Many of them had to open a special account for "conscience money" because they did not know how to account for the money they had received. An area employer confessed of theft and made reparation. A man who had circulated false checks gave himself up to the police. At the first hearing, the testimony of this man made an impression on the young judge.

"What are you doing at the present time?" he asked the accused.

"I am a member," said this disciple of Jesus, "of a gospel team. We go to other towns, where we sing and preach the good news."

"When you are holding another meeting like that here," said the judge, "let me know about it." He was informed, and the judge came to an evening of testimony.

At the trial the judge put him on probation for three months. The mother had prayed at a prayer meeting in the church for her unbelieving son. When she came home her son had in the meantime been saved.

Many pastors confessed that for years they had carried out their ministry only as a routine. Now, however, since they have been filled with the Spirit of God, not only their lives but also their ministry and their churches have become new.

From all over the country telephone calls came to Richard Grabke with requests for advice or for a team to be sent. Radio reporters and newspaper editors from New York and New Jersey, from Chicago and Alaska, asked for interviews and reports about the revival.

One newspaper reported: "The revival is an unmasking of Christians. Now you can see what Christians are really like." In this widespread movement several characteristics can be singled out. It is a wave of cleansing and of preparation for the second coming of the Lord.

This fact is highly significant. In the Indonesian revival too, strong expectation of the Lord's coming

came into prominence. Probably all the revivals, great
and small, which are at present appearing in the
world have an eschatological character. As in other
areas of revival, Bible verses about the humbling of
man play a decisive part. In Portland the words of
Isa. 57:15 are often quoted: "I dwell with Him who is
of a contrite and humble spirit to revive the spirit of
the humble, and to revive the heart of the contrite".

Many teams went out into the towns of Oregon in
order to evangelize. When the teams returned and
told their story, there were great times of rejoicing.
All of them reported that many people had received
their word and entrusted their lives to Jesus.

Chapter 23

TESTIMONIES FROM OREGON

The English expression "to give one's testimony" and the German phrase *"Zeugnis ablegen"* is meaningless to the world. In the language of believing Christians it means to report what Jesus means to one. Here are one or two short accounts.

Leonard Ravenhill used to say:

"The Christian who knows that he has been crucified with Christ has no ambition and therefore nothing to be jealous of. Such a Christian is not interested in recognition either. He therefore ceases the struggle to be recognized.

"A 'crucified Christian' is not tied to his possessions, and therefore he can abandon his worries about them. A crucified Christian makes no claim to rights and therefore he cannot suffer injustice. He is already dead to the world, and so no one can kill him."

James Bisel, a business man gave the following report:

"I have a contract to build nurses' homes, convalescent homes, schools and churches in the district of Portland.

"Last Good Friday evening (1972) God helped me to

confess everything to Him. My pride, my angry
temperament, my conceit and all my sinful habits had
to go. To be crucified with Christ, I had to recognize
this fact, before I could be filled with the Holy Spirit.
Only God can bring that about. I asked Him to fill me
with the Holy Spirit, and then I thanked Him. This
experience did not consist of overwhelming feelings
or accompanying signs; I simply laid claim to the
promises in the Bible. Since then I have been
experiencing a new life every day. I thank the Lord
that since this surrender of my life, He has been
using me and filling me every day anew with His
Holy Spirit."

Loretta Kovenz writes:
"It is hard to say how I should begin. It simply
surrounds a person. There is no beginning and no
end. I can only see the difference in all the
relationships. The church and all its members are
different from people. My relationship to all the
members of the church is new. I know that this comes
from the Holy Spirit. In all my life I have never
before had an experience like this. The sole ground
for this total change is a change of master. The Lord
lives His life in me, just as He does in the life of the
other believers too."

Mike Hill says:
"The Holy Spirit began to rule my life. I was a man
with worldly standards. Then I suddenly went
forward after a meeting. It was an act of faith. I
accepted the truth that Jesus had died to save me. It
was even harder for me to realize that I too had to
die. I surrendered to the Lord all my sinful habits and
the things that bound me. When I went to work the
next morning, I felt a great love towards all those
whom I met. A girl looked at me and said: 'What has
happened to you? You look so different!' Later another
Christian said to me: 'She still hasn't gotten over her

surprise. It would be better if you told her the reason for the change in you.' So I went to the place where the girl was working and told her: 'Charlotte, I have come to an end of leading my own life. Christ lives in me.' Unfortunately many people switch off when I speak of this great event in my life."

Patty Hill, Mike's wife, gives us the following description of the change in their lives:

"Before the Holy Spirit ruled our lives, we were already happily married. We did not have many tensions. Then in the revival Mike and I prayed for filling with the Holy Spirit and for 'the crucifixion of the flesh with its lusts.' At that hour my past was revealed to me. All my sins appeared before me. It was the Holy Spirit who made this revelation. I began to see our marriage, too, in a new light. Previously I had believed in the equal rights of man and wife. I became rebellious when Mike considered himself head of the family. I loved it when I was not simply overlooked, but needed. In the hour of our renewal, I recognized that it is the will of the Lord that I should submit myself. The Bible showed me that I must submit totally to my husband and that it is his task to love me as Christ loves His Church. That was the start of an indescribable life."

Chapter 24

MARKS OF THE REVIVAL

On the flight from Saskatoon to Minneapolis I asked Pastor McLeod: "What is the characteristic of this great revival? Can it be brought down to a common denominator?" "There are two main lines," he said. "Honesty before God and before men, and a mighty out-pouring of the love of God in the hearts of those who have repented."

Honesty—It was Killam, Alberta.
A group of young people had come from Neilburg, Saskatoon, to give their witness to about eighty people. This was a large group of young people from the area where the meeting was held. A minister who had come with ten young people began to weep when the Holy Spirit came over him. A youth leader publicly confessed that he was a shoplifter. He wanted to put the matter in order as quickly as possible. In the next few days he went to six shops and paid for what he had stolen. When a person becomes honest to God, he also becomes honest towards his neighbor.

Love—it was years ago in Mannheim.

There is a local saying there which means that ministers who have to work together in the same church often quarrel. This is not true in Germany alone. We find it on all continents. In the revival many reconciliations took place after the Spirit of God had convicted people. Pastors, elders, choir-masters and organists cleared away their petty jealousies and frictions.

An example from Mansfield, Ohio. A team came back from a weekend of ministry and reported:

"In one church all the leading members were at loggerheads. It had gone so far that a meeting was scheduled when the pastor was to be asked to resign. Because many were expecting a sensation, the meeting was very well attended. The team from Mansfield had the opportunity to give a report of the revival. The Spirit of God came over the church. The minister was the first to repent, and he then asked the leaders of the church to forgive him. The elders, deacons, and the choir-master, however, were also convicted by the spirit of repentance. They likewise humbled themselves before God, and then asked their pastor to forgive them. Instead of the dismissal of the pastor, God sent a new beginning for the whole church. Anger, tensions, hatred — removed by the love of God."

In the "Messenger," the monthly supplement of the Baptist Herald, the following summary of the marks of this revival appeared in April 1972:

1. It is a movement of repentance.
2. It is a movement of honesty.
3. It is a movement of love.

The picture of the revival is, however, so rich that even this triple division does not say everything. I have read and heard many testimonies. Again and again the same note comes through the reports:

Fulness of joy (Ps.16:11)

Peace like a river (Isa.48:18).

The life of those who have been touched by the Holy Spirit has been so changed, that those who carry this joy on their way through everyday life make a deep impression on people around them. Where the Bible is lived out, its message is proclaimed more loudly than it can be by words alone.

There are other characteristics, too. In the "Mid-West Memo," a magazine which is published in Regina, there is a remarkable statement. It reads: "There is no extreme emotionalism in evidence anywhere. A quiet non-charismatic work of the Holy Spirit is the order of every meeting."

This statement leads us to the secret of a balanced biblical revival. In other words, this revival in Canada cannot be identified with the highly emotional charismatic movement so-called. The revival is a gift of the Holy Spirit. Emotionalism is the activation of the psyche stirred up in a religious direction.

This brings us to a further characteristic of the revival — biblical moderation.

We have kept to the last the hardest part of all.

Death to one's own self — to be crucified with Christ, buried with Christ, risen again with Christ, given new life with Christ. That is the message of the Apostle Paul in Romans 6.

And now I will be an egoist. I ask the reader of this book to pray for me, that I may not only talk about this biblical truth, but practice it. To give oneself up, to submit one's own will to the will of God, to be crucified in a daily struggle, to be nothing.

This does not mean to be a weakling, but it means a change of command. If we ourselves are deeply concerned that God should send a revival to Europe to our own churches and our own lives, it will happen only by way of death.

He who dies to himself will live.